TABLE OF CONTENTS

INTRODUCTION

Peru has recently been described as a "country poised on the brink of collapse," by official Department of Defense reports.[1] Much of the responsibility for this condition has been attributed to one of the most radical Communist groups to appear on the world scene.

Peru's <u>Sendero Luminoso</u>, or as it is more commonly known, the Shining Path, has been labeled in many different ways. They have been referred to as revolutionaries and freedom fighters by their supporters. Their opponents have called them criminals, insurgents, guerrillas, and terrorists. However, there is no doubt concerning their fanaticism or willingness to use violence.

Their first act of violence occurred on May 17, 1980 when they burned all the ballot boxes at a rural polling station during an election.[2] Since that first act of violence, thousands of lives have been lost and billions of dollars worth of property damaged and destroyed.

However, unlike many guerrilla or insurgent

organizations, the Shining Path has been unconcerned about publicity, world opinion, or getting credit for their wanton acts of violence. Much of this is a result of the extremely secretive nature of Sendero Luminoso. However, they have also established a policy of propaganda by deed. They have shunned journalists and the media and consequently much of what is written is not always based on first hand knowledge or fact. Much of the information for this study is based on two short texts (one written in 1981 and the other in 1982), trial testimony of captured Senderists, an occasional communique, and two interviews with Abimael Guzman (one in September 1986 and the other in 1988).

Peru has become a major target in the war that the United States has declared on drugs. Consequently, U.S. interest in this organization is primarily focused on Sendero Luminoso's involvement with narcotics. While it appears they are not directly involved in the drug trade, they have been providing protection and security to both the peasants who grow the coca and the cocaine traffickers. It is estimated this activity provides Sendero Luminoso between $10 and 40 million a year in income.[3] An official with the

U.S. State Department pointed out that it is not possible to conduct counternarcotics operations in Peru without fighting the Shining Path.[4] If this country is to be effective in this war that we have declared on drugs, we must develop a comprehensive strategy for dealing with both the Sendero Luminoso and the counternarcotics problem in Peru because they are interrelated. Although not probable, the possibility exists that the United States could become involved in or stumble into another "dirty little war." Consequently, it is in our own self-interests that we learn as much as possible about this organization. That is the ultimate purpose of this study.

This paper will focus on the roots of the insurgency; its geographical, economic, and ethnic perspective will be discussed in detail. I will examine the rise of Sendero Luminoso, the origin of the movement, its development, and its philosophy. Following this I will analyze the threat Sendero Luminoso poses for the United States. The report will terminate with some conclusions.

ROOTS OF THE INSURGENCY

A basic understanding of the geography, the population, and the economy of Peru is necessary in order to comprehend the origins of this insurgency. The diversity within these three areas is a basic factor influencing the rise of Sendero Luminoso.

Peru is the fourth largest country in Latin America and is slightly smaller than the state of Alaska. Geographically it consists of three distinct regions. The coast constitutes 11 percent of the land and stretches approximately fourteen hundred miles from north to south in a narrow band fifty to one hundred miles wide. The region contains over fifty percent of the population and the country's five largest cities, to include Lima, the capital. This area contains the most productive agricultural lands, petroleum and mineral resources, and most of Peru's manufacturing capability.

The *sierra* or highlands contain the Andes, and constitute 24 percent of the total land area and occupy the rugged central portion of the country. This area contains approximately forty percent of the population, who earn their livelihood primarily from agriculture, though only a small percentage of the land is arable. Large deposits of minerals are located in this region, but the rugged terrain and lack of a transportation network hinder their exploitation.

The *montana* or Amazon basin comprises the remaining 65 percent of the country and less than 10 percent of the population. This area contains vast resource potential as well as substantial oil reserves which were discovered in the 1970s. However, the nearly impenetrable rain forest has kept this area almost totally isolated from the rest of the country. This isolation is best exemplified by the existence of an Indian tribe whose first contact with the outside world did not occur until the late nineteenth century and who continued to practice cannibalism until the 1970s.[5]

Peru as of 1990 had a population of twenty two million. It is projected to double within the next twenty-eight years. The characteristics of the population are important when viewed from the perspective of the roots of the insurgency.

Of primary importance are the ethnic distinctions. The latest figures indicate the population is 45 percent Indian, 37 percent Mestizo, 15 percent White, and 3 percent Black and Asiatic.

The Mestizo is a mixture of Indian and Hispanic ancestry who has to a large degree been integrated within the Hispanic society.

The Indian population is divided into two major groups by language--Quechua or Aymara, which were the languages of the Incas. They are also concentrated in the central and southern *sierra*. This portion of the population has generally not been integrated into the dominant Hispanic culture. Not only have they retained their own language, but also their own dress, culture, traditions, and outlook on life that is in conflict with that of the Hispanics who control the country.

This has led to what is known as the "Indian problem". There is a great deal of both prejudice against and fear of the Indian. This has existed since the Spanish conquest. Periodically over the last two centuries the Indians have revolted against this repression. The revolt of Tupac Amaru II in 1780 serves as an example of one of the largest and bloodiest Indian revolts in Latin America. These revolts and a Spanish requirement for labor have been used to justify the subjugation and exploitation of the Indians.

This exploitation has resulted in the Indians being almost totally separated from the land which they view as sacred. It resulted in the formation of a land tenure system during colonial times based on two distinct foundations. The first was latifundia, which meant large estates which were concentrated in the hands of the few wealthy, and the second was minifundia, which meant tiny parcels barely sufficient to feed one family. The last agricultural census highlights this problem. At that time, less than one-half of 1 percent of Peru's farms occupied 75 percent of the land; and the largest one thousand haciendas, larger than 42,000 acres, accounted for 60 percent of the arable land.[6] In contrast, 83 percent of the farms occupied less than 6 percent of the land and one-third of these were smaller than 2.5 acres.[7]

Thus we have the roots of the insurgency: a distinct ethnic population that has been historically exploited and feared, and has not been integrated into the society; a highly inequitable land distribution system that has resulted in the Indians being described as virtual slaves; and a distinct geographical area where this segment of society is concentrated. The area has been neglected and now serves as a base for the development of this insurgency.

Sendero Luminoso found fertile ground for their philosophy among the Indians and began to build a revolutionary base in the 1970s and to radicalize the Indian population.

It has been stated that "insurgencies are deeply rooted in individual cultures, in religious, racial and social differences".[8] These differences are readily apparent in Peru. They have served as the basis for Sendero Luminoso's initial appeal and acceptance, and have led to the rise of the Shining Path.

THE RISE OF SENDERO LUMINOSO

It has been apparent for some time that the social basis for revolution has existed within the country. Socialists and Communists have attempted to exploit it for forty years without success. It was not until the arrival of the right leader that an insurgent movement really took root.

Abimael Guzman provided the leadership that had been missing. He has been the primary force in Sendero Luminoso's ideological development as well as its chief strategist. He is now described as the "Fourth Sword of Marxism" whose work and ideological contributions compare with those of Marx, Lenin, and Mao.[9]

As a university student Guzman was involved in radical politics and was an active member of the Communist Party. He graduated with honors from the University of San Agustin with doctorate degrees in both law and philosophy. In 1962 he joined the faculty at the University of San Cristobal de Huamanga in Ayacucho in the southern *sierra*. He was described as "a theorist of the highest level" and a charismatic intellectual who attracted a loyal student, faculty, and community following.[10] During the 1960s, while at the university, he organized Communist party cells and was active in peasant land invasions in the Ayacucho region. During this time he also spent time in China on two separate occasions for military and political training.[11] These visits to China had a major impact on his ideological development.

Throughout the 1960s there were ideological disputes, fissures, and splits within the Peruvian Communist Party (PCP). Finally, in 1970 Guzman and his followers were expelled from the PCP for ideological heresy and "occultism".[12] It was at this juncture that Abimael Guzman and his followers formed the <u>Partido Comunista del Peru en el Sendero Luminoso de Mariategui</u> or the Shining Path.

During the 1970s Guzman and his followers laid the groundwork of Sendero Luminoso. Their entire effort was devoted to recruitment, organizing, and planning. Guzman, as the personnel director at the university in Ayacucho, was able to radicalize the faculty who in turn indoctrinated the student body which was 70-75 percent Indian in origin.[13] These young militants then returned to the communities of the *sierra* where they worked as teachers, social workers, and public servants. They developed the initial base of support for Sendero Luminoso and organized the party apparatus. Additionally, ancillery organizations such as trade unions, women's and students' groups, and the poor peasants movement were organized and developed throughout the country, but primarily in the *sierra* and the Indian slums of Lima. Sendero believed these organizations were necessary in order to mobilize the broad support of the masses. These efforts were successful primarily because of the almost total neglect of this area by the central government. The deep rooted historical Indian distrust of the government coupled with this official void provided fertile ground for Sendero's message and many potential supporters.

During this same time Guzman refined the ideology and philosophy of Sendero Luminoso. This ideological base was a synthesis of three major sources: the native socialism of Jose Carlos Mariategui who was the founder of the Peruvian Socialist Party, the works of Mao Zedung, and Incan mysticism and nationalism. He used Mao's ideology and revolutionary philosophy as the foundation. To this he applied a combination of socialist teachings of Mariategui and Incan mysticism. Guzman reinterpreted these principles as they applied to contemporary Peru. There are certain ideological differences, but those are beyond the scope of this paper.

Mao's primary appeal to Sendero Luminoso is "his insistence that a peasant-based, violent insurrection is the only way to install a dictatorship of the proletariat."[14] It is Guzman's belief that victory can only be achieved through armed struggle. This philosophy has led to the brutal, ruthless terrorist campaign that the Shining Path has directed against all who do not support their cause.

The organization also closely reflects Mao's perspective on both the state and social classes. Regarding social classes, Sendero, like Mao, has established its primary support among the poor peasants--in this case the Indian population. The enemies of the people in both ideologies are imperialism, large landowners, and the bureaucratic capitalists.[15] Sendero sees very little difference in any government which has recently existed in Peru -- they reject them all, as well as the various political parties. Like Mao, Sendero believes a "new democratic state" will be absolutely essential to bridge the gap between any current type of government and a socialist dictatorship of the proletariat.[16] There is no ideological divergence between Mao and Sendero as to who the "new democracy" incorporates, but there appears to be a practical difference. A mid-level Sendero leader said the following concerning the members of the "new democracy":

> First they will be given political
> reeducation, and if that fails, they
> will receive what we get now: dictator-
> ship, prison, . . . death. The genocide
> which we have accepted, they will have
> to accept.[17]

Guzman has adapted the philosophy of Mariategui as it relates to the Indian and even carried it beyond the borders of Peru. These tenets hold that political legitimacy is based on the perspective of the Indian (peasant) masses, not the white minority. The Indian community of the *sierra* will serve as the source and roots of a rejuvenated Andean society. According to Guzman the ultimate goal of the revolution is to include all Quechua speaking people of the region who will unite to establish a new state.[18]

This portion of Sendero's ideology also incorporates various aspects of Andean messianism which still remains strong among the rural peasants. Incan history promises a return to the Incan Golden Age. Sendero has used this element to its advantage on many occasions. In 1980 Sendero Luminoso used an old Incan legend to announce the beginning of its war. The morning after elections, which it opposed, dead dogs were discovered hanging from utility poles on one of Lima's busiest streets. Many thought it was the result of pranksters, but the peasants in the *sierra* understood its ominous meaning.

> According to a popular legend dating
> back to the Incas, which Indians in the
> region who have never heard of Mao can

easily recite, the dog is a companion
who follows, or leads, his master to the
grave. And so the peasants figured . . .
that wherever a hanging dog appeared,
someone was going to die, or be put to
death.[19]

Guzman has taken advantage of the peasants' beliefs in these superstitions and customs. He has developed and cultivated an image of genius and omnipresence which plays on these Indian legends in order to advance his cause.

From this ideological foundation, the Shining Path developed its political agenda. First and foremost was the creation of a "new state of workers and peasants." Additionally, Sendero has called for the elimination of all capitalistic institutions. They have called for the abolition of the banking system, foreign trade, currency, industry, and the national market economy; they have advocated the establishment of a village oriented economy based on barter.[20] This program is similar to what the Khmer Rouge sought to establish in Cambodia. These measures have been taken in a very limited way in some of the areas the Shining Path has "liberated". There can be no doubt that this program will move the area and the nation backward and destroy all elements of capitalism.

In May, 1980, Guzman concluded that the time had come to initiate the armed struggle and apply Mao's theories of armed revolution. He envisioned this struggle as lasting up to fifty years and consisting of the following five stages:

> (1) Agitation and armed propaganda to convert backward areas into a solid foundation for larger activities in the future. Occurred May, 1980-1981.
>
> (2) Attacks on the bourgeois state through systematic sabotage and initial regular guerrilla actions. Occurred throughout.
>
> (3) Generalized guerrilla warfare and violence that necessarily involves confrontations with the armed forces of the country. Occurred throughout 1983.
>
> (4) Conquest and expansion of the revolution's support base and the strengthening of the guerrilla army. Sendero Luminoso announced that it had achieved this stage in 1990.
>
> (5) Full-scale civil war that will lay siege to the cities and bring on the final collapse of the state.[21]

Since 1980, Sendero has waged a ruthless campaign of terrorism, bombings, and assassinations. Each year the level of violence has escalated. The appendix contains a selected chronology of some of these acts of terrorism. Since 1980, between 20,000 to 25,000 lives have been lost and $15 billion worth of property destroyed as a result of the terrorist activities of Sendero Luminoso.[22]

IMPLICATIONS FOR THE UNITED STATES

What impact does Sendero Luminoso have on the United States? On the surface the answer would appear to be none. Geopolitically Peru is of limited importance and this region poses no direct threat to our vital interests. However, this superficial assessment is not correct for several reasons.

The President's perspective sets the stage for describing this issue at the national level. The August, 1991, National Security Strategy of the United States, states that one of our national objectives and interests is to aid democratic institutions in combatting threats from aggression, coercion, insurgencies, subversion, terrorism, and illicit drug trafficking.[23] Thus our national security strategy provides the rationale for opposing Sendero Luminoso from the perspective of our war on drugs as well as supporting the democratically elected government of Peru.

There are several dimensions to this issue. The first

is the existence of a new world order. Since the end of

World War II, U.S. policy has been predicated on the concept

of containment of Communist expansion. This nation met the

Communist challenge in the political, economic, and military

arenas throughout the world over the last 45 years. On

several occasions this conflict manifested itself as

competition between the United States and Communists in the

Third World at the lower end of the spectrum of conflict.

Vietnam, El Salvador, and Nicaragua serve as primary examples

of this nation attempting to counter Communist influence.

As a result of this new world order and the relaxation

of tension and competition, our threat and justification for

involvement in a nation such as Peru has been greatly

reduced. Thus, it is in our national interests to adjust

policy accordingly.

What should United States' policy be concerning Peru and

the problems it is encountering as a result of Sendero

Luminoso and the drug war? There is no easy answer to this

question. Any action taken by this country concerning Peru

has potential pitfalls. There are those who believe we

should provide absolutely no support to the government of Peru because of its human rights violations. On the other hand, there are those who advocate major increases in U.S. support to fight the drug war, which in this case includes Sendero Luminoso.

Upon initial examination, my recommendation on a course of action would be very pragmatic -- no United States involvement. Our vital interests are not being threatened and the problems are so large and intractable as to almost defy solution. The ultimate solution to these problems requires long term internal action in the economic, social, and political arenas. Also some parallels can be drawn between Southeast Asia (Vietnam and Cambodia) twenty years ago and Peru today. The governments were corrupt, inefficient, and ineffective. They were unable to meet the needs of the people and thus lost their support and legitimacy. An insurgency moved to fill this void.

However, after more examination and reflection on the issues involved, doing nothing would be the worse course of action for several reasons. First, the current government was democratically elected by a majority of the Peruvian people on 10 June 1990. President Fujimori received 56.5 percent of the vote and carried 23 of Peru's 24 departments. Eighty percent of Peru's 10 million eligible voters cast their vote even though the Shining Path threatened death to all who voted.[24]

The new president inherited a government that was a virtual basket case. By all accounts, he is making some of the hard decisions that are necessary to bring about reform. The mandate he received from the Peruvian people clearly reflects their desire for democracy. They want to give a "new government" an opportunity to address Peru's problems. It is a U.S. national interest and objective to aid and support democratic institutions. Any alternative government, be it military, socialist, communist, or the Shining Path would certainly not be in either our best interest or that of the region.

Secondly, the United States is one of the major champions of human rights in the world. We only have to look at Cambodia and the slaughter of approximately one million people by the Khmer Rouge to understand the inhumanity of organizations like Sendero Luminoso. The Shining Path has embraced a similar philosophy and expressed open admiration

for this particular group. Since 1980, the Shining Path has

established a reputation for excessive violence, brutality,

and fanaticism. They have vowed to use genocide against

their opponents. We have a responsibility to preclude this,

if at all possible.

Finally, because of our unique relationship with the

nations of this hemisphere, the United States has a special

responsibility to them. They are our neighbors; they look to

us for guidance and assistance. Additionally, their

assistance and cooperation is necessary if we are to deal

with one of our major problems. Peru is a key point in our

war on drugs. Thus, it is mutually beneficial to assist one

another and work together in solving our problems.

We must balance these responsibilities with the

knowledge that we are not the world's policeman and that

there are limits to our power. Our involvement should take

the form of economic, social, political, and security

assistance which is directed toward treating the problems as

opposed to the symptoms. We need to promote economic

development, the growth of democratic institutions, and

social reform. Increased economic aid and aggressive implementation of provisions of both the Brady Plan and the Enterprise for the Americas Initiative (EAI) would be beneficial for Peru. The Brady Plan, which encourages agreements with commercial banks to restructure and reduce external debt, can help Peru in dealing with one of its most serious economic problems. The EAI would assist in promoting prosperity through liberalizing trade and investment policies which would stimulate economic growth. Also, efforts to provide nation building assistance should be increased.

Security assistance will also be a necessary element of our strategy. This effort needs to be focused on training and helping professionalize the Peruvian military. Widespread corruption and human rights violations have played right into the hands of Sendero Luminoso. The primary purpose of the military forces in this environment is to prevent the insurgent forces from disrupting legitimate political rule within the legal system. To do otherwise, alienates the very people whose support is necessary in order to defeat the insurgency.

For the last two years a fifteen-man Special Forces unit

has been training Peruvians in jungle warfare.[25] The State Department recently proposed an increase in this commitment of an additional fifty Special Forces instructors as part of a $94 million anti-drug program.[26] This is precisely the type of security assistance we need to provide Peru. It should be increased within reasonable limits, but extreme caution and care must be exercised in this regard. We must always be vigilant against being drawn into another nasty little war that we can not control or win. Under no circumstances should commitment of U.S. conventional military forces be considered for reasons previously discussed. Any action of this nature would play right into the hands of Sendero Luminoso. Our strategy needs to be dedicated toward ameliorating the root causes of this conflict by promoting economic development, social reform, and the growth and strengthening of democratic institutions.

CONCLUSIONS

Sendero Luminoso is a one-of-a-kind organization that owes its existence to the confluence of some unique circumstances. The region's cultural, geographical, and political isolation were major factors in the development of this organization. The almost total disregard by the government for the needs of the people of this region, combined with a sick economy, provided fertile ground for a charismatic leader who understood the people, history, and the nature of the problems.

Sendero is a relatively young organization which has made great strides in a short period of time. It poses a serious threat to the continued existence of the democratic government which now governs Peru. Should Sendero succeed tens of thousands of people will perish.

The principle factors which gave rise to this organization were social, economic, and political. Consequently, any solution must address these in order to succeed. General Adrian Huaman Centeno, who was military commander of the Ayacucho region in 1983, initiated a program of positive action to improve the community and the life of the peasants. He succeeded in almost completely eliminating Sendero from its birthplace. Three days after he made the following statement he was relieved:

> Here the solution is not military, because if it
> had been military I would have resolved it in minutes.
> If it were a question of destroying Ayacucho, it would

not exist for half an hour...We would be done with the
problem. But that is not the answer. What is happening
is that we are talking about human beings from the
forgotten pueblos who have been crying out for 160
years, and no one paid any attention to them. Now
we are reaping the result.[27]

If this fledgling democracy is to survive, Peru must

institute changes and address the inequalities of the society

or Sendero Luminoso will continue to exist. At this point,

neither the government nor Sendero Luminoso has the

capability to win this conflict. Thus, the prognosis is

continued bloodshed.

Selected Incident Chronology

August 1981 - Bombed the US Embassy, the Bank of America, the Coca Cola bottler, and a dairy product firm associated with the Carnation Company, all in Lima.

July 1982 - Threw two dynamite bombs at the US Embassy and set off bombs at three private businesses, injuring three people.

May 1983 - Blew up 10 electrical powerline towers in a coordinated attack that blacked out Lima, and set off over 30 bombs during the confusion, causing over $27 million in damage.

August 1984 - Burned an evangelical church run by US missionaries in southeastern Ayacucho Department.

December 1985 - Set off a bomb in the Lima airport parking lot, killing a child and four other people.

March 1986 - Assassinated three provincial mayors by shooting them in the head in the town of Chacra Pampas.

June 1986 - Over 200 alleged Sendero Luminoso (SL) members killed in a prison riot and the subsequent Government attempt to retake the prison.

June 1986 - Bombed Cuzco-Machu Picchu tourist train, killing 8 (including 1 American) and wounding 40 (including 9 Americans).

July 1986 - Bombed the Soviet Embassy in Lima.

January 1987 - Attacked Indian Embassy.

February 1987 - Bombed seven banks and burned a textile factory in Lima.

April 1987 - Assaulted a busload of military and civilian passengers in Huanacavelica, killing 13 people.

April 1987 - Attacked the North Korean Commercial Mission in Lima, injuring at least three people.

May 1987 - Conducted a major series of bombings, blacking out most of Lima. Targets included the Ministries of Agriculture, Labor, and Transportation and Communication.

September-October 1987 - Detonated car bomb near Congress Building, causing partial blackout in Lima. Killed over 40 civilians in attacks against 2 towns in Tocache Province.

June 1988 - Two US Agency for International Development subcontractors were killed while traveling near Huancayo, Peru, an area controlled by the SL.

March 1990 - Launched a major offensive. Attacked two Andean villages, killing 74 peasants, many of them children.

July 1991 - Executed three Japanese agronomists and blew up research laboratories.

January 12, 1992 - Shot down U.S. provided helicopter on anti-drug mission. Three Americans (civilians) were killed.

ENDNOTES

1.   Defense Logistics Agency, <u>The Shining Path and the Future of Peru</u>, by Gordon H. McCormick, March 1990, 1, DTIC, Ad-A223 p. 249.

2.   Department of State, Office of the Secretary of State/Coordinator for Counter-Terrorism, <u>Sendero Luminoso (Shining Path)</u> ([Washington, D.C.]: U.S. Department of State, Office of the Secretary of State/Coordinator for Counter-Terrorism, 1989), p. 49.

3.   Christopher Marquis, "Plagued by a host of ills, Peru may be beyond help," <u>Philadelphia Inquirer</u>, 19 December 1991, p. E1.

4.   Harry Anderson, Robert Parry, Spencer Reiss, Michael L. Smith, and Douglas Waller, "The Next Nasty War?" <u>Newsweek</u>, 21 May 1990, p. 36.

5.   Daniel M. Masterson, <u>Militarism and Politics in Latin America</u> (New York: Greenwood Press, 1991), p. 5.

6.   <u>Ibid.</u>,p. 6.

7.   <u>Ibid.</u>

8.   Robert B. Ash, "Sendero Luminoso and the Peruvian Crisis," <u>Conflict Quarterly</u>, Summer 1985, p. 19.

9.   Defense Logistics Agency, <u>The Shining Path and the Future of Peru</u>, p. 3.

10.   Masterson, p. 276.

11.   <u>Ibid.</u>

12. Defense Logistics Agency, <u>The Shining Path and the Future of Peru</u>, p. 4.

13. Masterson, p. 277.

14. Andrew Wheat, "Shining Path's 'Fourth Sword' Ideology," <u>Journal of Political and Military Sociology</u>, Summer 1990, p. 47.

15. <u>Ibid.</u>, p. 49.

16. <u>Ibid.</u>, p. 48.

17. <u>Ibid.</u>

18. Rand Corp., <u>The Shining Path and Peruvian Terrorism</u>, by Gordon H. McCormick, January 1987, p. 8, Rept P-7297.

19. Ash, p. 21.

20. Rand Corp., <u>The Shining Path and Peruvian Terrorism</u>, p. 7.

21. Henry Dietz, "Peru's Sendero Luminoso As A Revolutionary Movement," <u>Journal of Political and Military Sociology</u>, Summer 1990, p. 131.

22. Gustavo Gorriti, "The War Of The Philosopher-King," <u>The New Republic</u>, 18 June 1990, p.16.

23. U.S. Executive Department, <u>National Security Strategy of the United States</u> ([Washington, D.C.]: Executive Department, August 1991), p.4.

24. David P. Werlich, "Fujimori and the 'Disaster' in Peru," <u>Current History</u>, February 1991, p. 81.

25. Clara Bingham, Charles Lane, and Brook Larmer, "Peru: Into the Cross-fire," <u>Newsweek</u>, 19 August 1991, p. 29.

26. <u>Ibid</u>.

27. Masterson, p. 283.

BIBLIOGRAPHY

BOOKS

Becket, Ian F.W. and John Pimlott. <u>Armed Forces and Modern Counter-Insurgency</u>. New York: St. Martins Press, 1985.

Masterson, Daniel M. <u>Militarism and Politics in Latin America</u>. New York: Greenwood Press, 1991.

Rapoport, David C., ed. <u>Inside Terrorist Organizations</u>. New York: Columbia University Press, 1988.

Rubin, Barry, ed. <u>The Politics of Terrorism: Terror As A State and Revolutionary Strategy</u>. Washington, D.C.: Foreign Policy Institute of The Johns Hopkins University, 1989.

Ware, Lewis B., Stephen Blank, Lawrence E. Grinter, Jerome W. Klingman, Thomas P. Ofcansky, and Bynum E. Weathers. <u>Low Intensity Conflict in the Third World</u>. Maxwell Air Force Base, Alabama: Air University Press, 1988.

MAGAZINES

Anderson, Harry, Robert Parry, Spencer Reiss, Michael L. Smith, and Douglas Walker. "The Next Nasty War?" <u>Newsweek</u>, 21 May 1990, pp. 36-37.

Ash, Robert B. "Sendero Luminoso and the Peruvian Crisis." <u>Conflict Quarterly</u>, Summer 1985, pp. 19-31.

Bingham, Clara, Charles Lane, and Brook Larmer. "Peru: Into the Cross-fire." <u>Newsweek</u>, 19 August 1991, pp. 29-30.

Bourque, Susan C. and Kay B. Warren. "Democracy Without Peace: The Cultural Politics of Terror in Peru." <u>Latin American Research Review</u>, 1989, pp. 7-34.

"Clergy Targeted In Peru?" <u>Christian Century</u>, 10-17 July
1991, pp. 681-682.

Dietz, Henry. "Peru's Sendero Luminoso As A Revolutionary
Movement." <u>Journal of Political and Military Sociology</u>,
Summer 1990, pp. 123-150.

Gorriti, Gustavo. "The War Of The Philosopher-King." <u>The
New Republic</u>, 18 June 1990, pp. 15-22.

Kirk, Robin. "Oh What A Lovely Drug War In Peru." <u>The
Nation</u>, 30 September 1991, pp. 371-376.

_____. "Shining Path Is Gaining in Peru." <u>The Nation</u>,
29 April 1991, pp. 552-556.

Lane, Charles, Peter Katel, Brook Larmer, and Douglas Waller.
"The Newest War." <u>Newsweek</u>, 6 January 1992, pp. 18-23.

Palmer, David Scott. "Peru's Persistent Problems." <u>Current
History</u>, January 1990, pp. 5-8, 31-34.

_____. "Rebellion in Rural Peru." <u>Comparative
Politics</u>, January 1986, pp. 127-146.

Rosenberg, Tina. "Guerrilla Tourism." <u>The New Republic</u>, 18
June 1990, pp. 15-22.

Vogel, Tom Jr. "The 'Karate Kid' Meets the Shining Path."
<u>Commonweal</u>, 11 January 1991, pp. 9-11.

_____. "The Lawless Road In Peru." <u>Commonweal</u>, 25
October 1991, pp. 611-612.

Werlich, David P. "Fujimori and the 'Disaster' in Peru."
<u>Current History</u>, February 1991, pp. 61-64, 81-83.

_____. "Peru: The Shadow of the Shining Path."
Current History, February 1984, pp. 78-82, 90.

Wheat, Andrew. "Shining Path's 'Fourth Sword' Ideology."
Journal of Political and Military Sociology, Summer 1990,
pp. 41-55.

"Why Are We In Peru?" The Nation, 14 May 1990, p. 653.

NEWSPAPERS

Brooke, James. "Marxist Revolt Flourishing In the
Shantytowns of Peru." New York Times, 11 November 1991,
pp. A1-A6.

Cohen, Roger. "Cocaine Rebellion." Wall Street Journal, 17
January 1989, p. 1+.

Marquis, Christopher. "Plagued by a host of ills, Peru may
be beyond help." Philadelphia Inquirer, 19 December 1991,
p. E1+.

Smith, Michael L. "Peruvian Rebel Offers Grim Prophecy."
Washington Post, 19 August 1988, p. A10.

DOCUMENTS

Defense Logistics Agency. Insurgency In Peru: The Shining
Path. By Major James V. Huston, USMC. 11 May 1988.
DTIC,AD-B132 589.

Defense Logistics Agency. The Shining Path and the Future of
Peru. By Gordon H. McCormick. March 1990. DTIC, AD-A223
249.

Foreign Affairs Center. The U.S. and the Politics of
Conflict in a Developing Nation. By Todd R.Greentree.
October 1990. Paper No. 4.

Rand Corporation. The Shining Path and Peruvian Terrorism.
By Gordon H. McCormick. January 1987. Rept P-7297.

U.S. Department of State. Office of the Secretary of
State/Coordinator for Counter-Terrorism. Sendero Luminoso
(Shining Path). [Washington, D.C.]: United States
Department of State, Office of the Secretary of
State/Coordinator for Counter-Terrorism, 1989.

U.S. Executive Department. National Security Strategy of the
United States. [Washington, D.C.]: Executive Department,
August 1991.

www.ingramcontent.com/pod-product-compliance
Lightning Source LLC
Chambersburg PA
CBHW080740290526
45790CB00008B/3267